JESUS REALLY SAID THAT?

ISBN: 978-1-943929-11-5

All Scripture quotations are taken from the NKJV unless noted otherwise.

Cover design: Teresa Sommers

Layout design: Kristi Yoder

Illustrations: Gavin Miles

Printed in the USA

Seventh printing: November 2022

Published by:
TGS International
P.O. Box 355
Berlin, Ohio 44610 USA
Phone: 330-893-4828
Fax: 330-893-4893
www.tgsinternational.com

JESUS REALLY SAID THAT?

Five teachings of Jesus that might surprise you

GARY MILLER

TABLE OF CONTENTS

CHAPTER ONE

LAKESIDE BELIEVERS FELLOWSHIP

Jeremy leaned back in his seat savoring the finale to his favorite part of the service. All week he had looked forward to Sunday morning at Lakeside Believers Fellowship, and he knew it was partly due to that first hour of praise. His toe instinctively tapped as the worship music washed over him. He used the time to pray, his closed eyes ignoring the crowd swaying to the tempo and the lyrics gliding across the wide, center-stage screens. No doubt, Lakeside's worship team had talent, and Jeremy found the experience a wonderful way to unwind after a tough week and get his focus back on God.

As the music ended, the auditorium lights dimmed and a spotlight focused on Pastor Mike as he stepped to the microphone for prayer.

"Thank you, God, for your awesome power. There is no one like you!" The large sanctuary resounded with exclamations of praise while a lone guitar strummed softly in the background.

"Lord, help us to see your glory. You are so good to us. Father, we aren't worthy, but make us worthy in the name of Jesus. Amen." The crowd settled back into their seats, and Jeremy's hand reached over for Alicia's as they shared a smile. They knew God was in control and leading them in their Christian walk.

Jeremy and Alicia hadn't always attended

Welcome to
Lakeside Believers Fellowship

Lakeside. As he listened to Pastor Mike, Jeremy's mind reviewed the past few years. So much had happened since high school graduation. His family had a history of faithful service to their country, so enlisting in the armed services had seemed the next logical step. But looking back, Jeremy knew he had joined for a deeper reason. He had wanted to be a part of something larger than himself, something providing solutions to the world's problems.

The television and newspapers were constantly spewing out a flood of unsettling information. Everywhere he looked there was discord and conflict—corporations taking advantage of the worker, the rich abusing the poor, and foreign governments causing starvation and poverty for their own selfish political gain. So much was wrong, and he had wanted to help make things right.

And then there were those radical Muslims. The stories of men torturing innocent people, assuming they were doing the will of Allah, was too much. Something had to be done! These deranged people needed to be stopped, and who else could put an end to this nonsense but the U.S. military? So Jeremy had joined the U.S. Army, serving part of his time in the Middle East.

He had gone assuming the United States was right and had the answers, but he returned home with major questions. Can you force men to change? Will more bombs and guns really create world peace? Jeremy had enlisted believing America had been blessed by God, was driven by a higher set of morals, and had a divine responsibility to assist the downtrodden. But his time in the service and interaction with other cultures had shown him that Americans were very much like the rest of the world.

After returning home from the military and marrying Alicia, his high school sweetheart, Jeremy's life had spun out of control. National superiority, the great truth he had leaned on, had let him down, and Alicia had looked on with dismay as Jeremy struggled. She watched him turn to alcohol and finally drugs, attempting to relieve his disillusionment. For months she feared for his sanity and worried that he might take his own life. And then someone had invited them to Lakeside Believers Fellowship.

Jeremy had grown up assuming he was a Christian, but had never actually made a public confession of Christ. He had shied away from people who seemed "too spiritual," but now, dependent on drugs and alcohol, he felt there was little to lose.

The people at Lakeside had been very friendly, and Jeremy knew he would never forget the love and acceptance he had felt from this church during that dark time in his life. They had reached out to him with open arms, and it had been just what he needed.

Lakeside was a large church with many programs, one of which ministered to individuals struggling with substance abuse. Jeremy had always had an interest in history, and one of the leaders had helped him enroll in a local university. Now, with just one more year of schooling and good prospects for employment as a history teacher, Jeremy and Alicia felt that the Lord had brought them here. They made a public confession of Christ, became active in a midweek Bible study, and began pouring their lives into Lakeside Believers Fellowship. The people and preaching were great, the music program second to none. As Jeremy turned his mind back toward Pastor Mike's message, it seemed his life was finally back on track.

CHAPTER TWO

JESUS—DO I REALLY KNOW HIM?

I want to personally welcome all the visitors today," Pastor Mike began. "Here at Lakeside Believers Fellowship we want you to feel at home, and if there is anything we can do to make your experience more enjoyable, let us know. A vibrant church is one in which everyone feels included and fulfilled. There is so much negativity in our world, and we want your time here to be positive. Like an oasis in a dry land, we want you to experience all the blessing and joy that the Lord has for you. When you exit through those doors, we want you to feel you've received a personal hug from God the Father! He loves you and cares about how you feel."

Jeremy smiled as he listened to Pastor Mike's enthusiastic welcome. *This is why our church is so large and continues to grow,* he thought. *People need to feel good about themselves and understand that God loves them. I'm glad we have a pastor who under-stands how people feel and wants to make their worship experience enjoyable and even fun!*

But suddenly, like a bolt of lightning, a statement from last Wednesday night's Bible study flashed through his mind, an unwelcome intrusion on his warm and fuzzy thoughts. Their study group had been working through the Gospel of John when they came across some strange words of Jesus: "Whoever eats My flesh and drinks My blood has eternal life, and I will raise him up at the last day."[1]

"I don't understand!" one young man had exploded. "Jesus knew that saying this was going to upset people. Why didn't He explain what He meant? If He was trying to get people to follow Him, why would He say things in a way that

---
[1] John 6:54

would cause them to walk away? Didn't Jesus want His church to grow?"

An intense discussion had followed, but what flashed through Jeremy's mind now was the question, "Didn't Jesus want His church to grow?"

Growth was what Lakeside was all about. They had seminars on church growth, graphs in the hallway that showed projected church growth, and every Sunday Pastor Mike encouraged them to bring visitors. Why did Jesus say things that made people walk away?

Jeremy glanced over at Alicia, who was obviously enjoying the message, and tried to push these questions from his mind. Of course Jesus wanted His church to grow. But why did He make statements that sounded a lot like cannibalism? Is that how you build a church? And just how would Jesus be regarded as a modern-day pastor? He started with twelve disciples, and by the time of His crucifixion was down to eleven. Even those weren't exactly loyal when the going got tough.

Jeremy didn't hear much of Pastor Mike's message that Sunday. His mind began to wrestle with this man, Jesus. Jeremy had publicly proclaimed that he loved Jesus, but how much about Him did he really understand?

If Jesus were a pastor in America today, what would His church look like? Would He be like Pastor Mike, attempting to help each person feel good about his or her church experience? Or would He give some messages so serious and challenging that many seekers would never return?

Jeremy felt a trickle of sweat tracing its way down his back. It was an unsettling feeling, similar to what he had experienced in the Middle East when first having doubts about his military involvement. He had been so sure that America was right. Was he wrong about Jesus as well? How well did he really know Jesus?

As a history lover, Jeremy thoroughly enjoyed research. But if he started to dig, would he like what he found?

Jeremy listened silently as Alicia chatted on the way home. She commented on several things that had impressed her about Pastor Mike's message, but suddenly she became aware of Jeremy's silence.

"What's bothering you, Jeremy? I noticed you kind of zoned out during the service, and you don't normally go straight to the car afterward. Is something wrong?"

"I just got to thinking about the difference between Pastor Mike and Jesus. Jesus seemed to preach things that repelled people, and I realized today that Pastor Mike would never do that."

Alicia's heart froze. They had come so far, and Lakeside Believers Fellowship had helped so much. Was Jeremy heading back down a negative path toward depression and disillusionment? Alicia was determined to avoid going back.

"Jeremy, that isn't fair! Look how much good Pastor Mike and Lakeside are doing, and how they have blessed us! Jesus lived in a completely different time and culture. We have no idea how He would preach today."

"You're right, Alicia, but I have been having some doubts. We have been blessed, and I appreciate Pastor Mike, but I want to take a closer look at the words and life of Jesus. I feel I don't understand Him or His message very well. I feel like I was misled by patriotism and the military, and I don't want to be hoodwinked again."

They were silent the rest of the way home as both focused on their fears. Alicia was fearful that this brief but pleasant interlude in their married life was coming to an end, and Jeremy that he had committed to something that might be hollow at its core. Arriving home, dinner was forgotten, but from their continued discussion they ultimately arrived at a consensus. They agreed on three points:

1. They would pray fervently for direction as they started looking closely at the teachings of Jesus.

2. Jeremy would research the early church and try to get a picture of how the early Christians interpreted Jesus' words.

3. They would continue to be a part of and an encouragement to Lakeside Believers Fellowship while they searched for truth.

CHAPTER THREE

HEARING AND DOING

Jeremy was a man of passion and resolve, and he lost no time in beginning his search. Early Monday morning found him opening the book of Matthew, notepad in hand, coffee by his side, eagerly starting down a path of discovery. Staying focused during morning devotions had previously been difficult, but with a mission of investigating this Jesus, Jeremy felt eager and energized. Who was He and what was His primary message? Even the Beatitudes, statements that had bored him as a child in Sunday school, seemed fresh and exciting. As he read, he jotted down phrases and thoughts that stood out to him. It didn't take him long to realize this wasn't going to be a quick or easy study.

The Sermon on the Mount was chock full of powerful statements! Why hadn't he noticed them before? Jeremy tried to read as though he had never seen the material before. He noted verses where Jesus warned against lust[1] and where He stressed the permanence of marriage.[2] He wondered what Jesus meant by saying a person should never swear,[3] or when He said we should give to everyone who asks.[4] He jotted down the reference where Jesus commanded His followers to love their enemies.[5] What could all this mean? How could a person put all this into practice and still survive in the world? He would need to give more thought to this.

On the second morning, Jeremy came across a verse that stopped him in his tracks. It was just a little passage, but somehow reading it as though Jesus were actually speaking directly to him made the verse come alive. And

[1] Matthew 5:28
[2] Matthew 5:31–32
[3] Matthew 5:33–37
[4] Matthew 5:42
[5] Matthew 5:43–47

the theological implications shook him to the core.

It was at the end of the Lord's prayer, and it simply said, "But if you do not forgive men their trespasses, neither will your Father forgive your trespasses."[6] Jesus was clearly saying that forgiveness—Jeremy's forgiveness—was conditional. Unless Jeremy was willing to forgive others' sins toward him, God wasn't going to forgive him either. Jeremy was shocked!

If there was one thing Jeremy had been taught at Lakeside Believers Fellowship, it was that salvation and forgiveness of sins was by faith alone in Jesus Christ. Every Sunday Pastor Mike in some way emphasized that a man's salvation was dependent only upon that man's faith in Jesus. God knew we couldn't live "good" enough to earn our salvation, and Jesus came to cover our unrighteousness with His righteousness. All a man needed to do was receive Jesus into his heart, and from that point on the blood of Jesus covered his life. This had been made clear when Jeremy was received as a member at Lakeside.

And yet Jesus was saying something entirely different.

---

[6] Matthew 6:15

If I choose to not forgive someone, even though I say I believe in Jesus, I will not be forgiven? Jeremy sat back in his chair and looked out the window. The sun was just coming up, and he would need to leave for work soon. But this little verse was unsettling. Salvation is conditional? Was he understanding it correctly? Weren't there other verses in the Bible that said all a man needed to do was receive Jesus into his heart? Or was it possible that obedience could be an important, vital requirement?

Heading off to work, Jeremy continued to think about this question, and that evening he began searching the Scriptures in earnest. He was astounded at what he found. Repeatedly Jesus emphasized that He was much more interested in what a man did than in his stated belief. Jesus often talked about the importance of a man's works.

Jeremy did a word search on the familiar phrase they heard each Sunday, "We are saved by faith alone." To his great astonishment, he couldn't find that phrase anywhere in the Bible. And even more surprisingly, the only passage he found using similar words said just the opposite. In the book of James the writer concluded a discourse on the topic of faith and works by saying, "You see then that a man is justified by works, and not by faith only."[7]

Jeremy had thought that human works were a bad thing—something people with poor doctrine did in a vain attempt to be saved. But as he went from reference to reference, he repeatedly found obedience as something good, an obvious identifier of those who are born again. Somehow Jeremy had come to believe that good works were a denial of Christ's victory on the cross. But it was clear that Jesus and His apostles taught something completely different.

But the real stunner came at the end of the seventh chapter of Matthew. After all those difficult commands in the Sermon on the Mount, Jesus said that many who thought He was their Lord would receive a tremendous shock on the Day of Judgment.

"Alicia, come here. Have you ever thought about this verse? Jesus says that many people will come to Him on Judgment Day and feel confident they are saved. They will believe they'd had a genuine relationship with Christ and had worked for Him, but Jesus will say He doesn't even know them!"

Their waiting breakfast forgotten, they read on

---

[7] James 2:24

as Jesus told a little story explaining who these surprised people will be. He told of two men who had built houses. The first dug down deep and built his on a rock. When the storm came, his house stood firm because it was anchored to a rock. Jesus said this builder is like a man who hears what Jesus says and goes out to do it. But the second man built his house on sand, and when the floodwaters rose and the wind blew, his house was demolished. Jesus said this builder is like a man who hears His teachings but doesn't obey.[8]

Jeremy and Alicia sat in stunned silence. They both remembered singing about this account in Sunday school but had never noticed the powerful import of what Jesus was saying. Finally Alicia spoke in a subdued voice. "So Jesus is saying that those who don't live out what He taught will be surprised on the Day of Judgment?"

Turning to the back of his Bible, Jeremy pointed to a passage he had found earlier. "Yes, according to what we're finding. This passage agrees with the verse regarding the judgment. Listen to this:

> And I saw the dead, small and great, standing before God, and books were opened.

---

[8] Matthew 7:24–27

And another book was opened, which is the Book of Life. And the dead were judged according to their works, by the things which were written in the books. The sea gave up the dead who were in it, and Death and Hades delivered up the dead who were in them. And they were judged, each one according to his works."[9]

Jeremy turned a page in his notepad. Across the top he wrote, "Questions for Pastor Mike," and then he started a list.

1. If a man's works do not matter, then why does the Bible say we will be judged by them?

---

[9] Revelation 20:12–13

CHAPTER FOUR

HAPPINESS OR HOLINESS?

Jeremy's search had begun with a few simple questions. "If Jesus were the lead pastor of Lakeside Believers Fellowship, what kind of a pastor would He be? What type of sermons would He preach, and how would listeners feel after one of His messages?" Early Monday morning during his second week of study, Alicia walked into the room bringing Jeremy a fresh cup of coffee.

"Anything new this morning? I started going through my Bible after our discussion last week, and I keep finding more verses regarding the importance of obedience. There are so many places where the New Testament writers clearly state that a follower of Jesus will have an intense desire to obey Him. Most of us assume we are obedient, but we haven't given Jesus' words much attention. Why haven't we taken some of these passages more seriously? I didn't realize Jesus even said some of these things!"

Jeremy sipped his coffee before replying. "I know what you mean, and I'm not sure I have an answer. But one thing is becoming clear. If Jesus were our pastor, I suspect Lakeside's preaching would be very different."

"But is that fair, Jeremy? We have always enjoyed Pastor Mike's messages. He bases everything on the Bible, and I think everyone goes away refreshed, excited, and feeling better than when they came."

Laying down his Bible, Jeremy tipped his head back and stared at the ceiling. What was different about the message of Jesus? It was true, Pastor Mike gave interesting and enthusiastic sermons. He always provided Bible verses that supported what he was saying, and everyone enjoyed his teaching. So what was different?

"You're right, Alicia. Pastor Mike's sermons are inspiring and enjoyable. I have never heard others say they didn't like one of his messages. But that may be the difference. Jesus' message wasn't universally appreciated. His teachings made some men angry, and others walked away and didn't come back."[1]

---

[1] John 6:66

Alicia frowned at her coffee before responding. "But how could a pastor grow a church if he didn't preach sermons people liked? What good would it do to offend people and have them walk away?"

"That's just it, Alicia! As you read what Jesus said and how He said it, He obviously loved people and had their best interests in mind. But He didn't say things just to make them feel good. He spoke truth, even when He knew it would hurt. He seemed more interested in how they lived than in how they felt."

Jeremy glanced at his watch. "I've got to get moving or I'll be late for work again." Grabbing his coffee, he headed out the door. "Let's talk more about this tonight."

Alicia sat in silence for a few minutes. Was there a difference between Jesus' teachings and Pastor Mike's sermons at Lakeside? The initial thought angered her. Pastor Mike had done so much for them, and Alicia didn't appreciate hearing him criticized. She sat for a moment and then retrieved her Bible, quickly thumbing back through her sermon notes from the past few months, hoping to prove her husband wrong.

That evening when Jeremy returned, the discussion continued.

"I felt bad today about my comments regarding Pastor Mike," Jeremy began. "He has done a lot for us, and I really enjoy his messages."

"I like listening to him as well, Jeremy, but after you left this morning, I reviewed my sermon notes. If I were to summarize Pastor Mike's messages, as good as they are, I must admit that almost all of them would fit under one basic heading. There are a couple of exceptions, but most would follow the theme, 'How to be saved and make this life and the next more enjoyable!' Maybe this is why we like his messages—they make us feel good!"

"But, Alicia, Jesus' message was completely different! His message was a sober call to repent of our past, give up personal rights, and completely surrender to Him. He clearly said in a verse I just read that any man who is not willing to give up himself and everything he has cannot be His disciple![2] While the message of Jesus centers on transforming people, Lakeside focuses on the importance of each person's happiness—almost like our culture which seems obsessed with ensuring that each moment is enjoyed and exciting. People yearn for a state of perpetual enjoyment, and woe to the person who

---

[2] Luke 14:33

brings bad news, who is boring, or who tells us that something in our lives needs to change."

As Jeremy and Alicia continued to discuss the message of Jesus, they realized that marketing such a message to a fun-loving society wasn't easy. Pastors were in a difficult dilemma. The Apostle Paul had said that the preaching of the cross is foolishness to the world.[3] That simply meant people were not going to like it. So what was a pastor to do? How could he get a fun-loving, entertainment-seeking, self-centered crowd to love a self-denying message?

"Our culture has probably influenced us more than we think," said Jeremy soberly. "We are accustomed to being entertained, and the main goal of entertainment is to please the crowd. But the main purpose of authentic Christianity should be to please the Lord. That means giving up our rights. We don't like that message! So this is the question, Alicia: How is a pastor supposed to market a message that is repulsive to his listeners?

"It's almost as though we are trying to repackage the product!" Jeremy continued. "Give Jesus a makeover and change Him into an exuberant

---

[3] 1 Corinthians 1:18

and entertaining man who wants, above all, for you to be happy. But I haven't found anything in the Bible that shows the first Christians enticing people to Jesus by packaging Christianity as an eye-catching option. Their message required a man to repent of his past and start living a holy life."

Flipping through his Bible, Jeremy continued. "Listen to these words from Peter:

> Therefore gird up the loins of your mind, be sober, and rest your hope fully upon the grace that is to be brought to you at the revelation of Jesus Christ; as obedient children, not conforming yourselves to the former lusts, as in your ignorance; but as He who called you is holy, you also be holy in all your conduct, because it is written, 'Be holy, for I am holy.' And if you call on the Father, who without partiality judges according to each one's work,

conduct yourselves throughout the time of your stay here in fear."[4]

Alicia sat for a moment before responding. "Wow! So it wasn't just Jesus who emphasized holiness. Those are powerful words. I wonder how our congregation would react to this kind of message?"

"Probably just like the crowd that Jesus preached to. A few received it, but many walked away. Telling people they need to change and that they need to deny themselves will always be difficult."

Jeremy leaned back and thought a moment before continuing. "Maybe I am missing something, but a thought keeps going through my mind. Jesus was obviously more interested in holiness than in happiness."

Before Jeremy went to bed that evening, he flipped back to his page titled "Questions for Pastor Mike" and added the second item to his list.

1. If a man's works do not matter, then why does the Bible say we will be judged by them?

2. Why do we teach and focus so much on personal happiness and so little on personal holiness?

---

[4] 1 Peter 1:13–17

CHAPTER FIVE

A KINGDOM THAT DOESN'T FIGHT?

For the last several weeks Jeremy had been reading the Scriptures differently than ever before. Each morning he tried to read as though the material were new and unfamiliar. This wasn't easy. Some passages he had heard all his life, and a few he had memorized as a child in Sunday school. But even though reading like this was difficult, he had never found anything so fulfilling. It was like uncovering a new treasure each morning, and he looked forward to it. Like reading a good mystery book, he had trouble laying the Bible down when it was time to go to work or to bed. Alicia was amazed at this dramatic change and couldn't help commenting.

"Do you realize we have hardly watched TV for the past two weeks? You didn't even watch last night's football game!"

Jeremy looked up with a funny expression. He had completely forgotten the game. Something else of greater value had captured his mind, and Alicia could tell from the look in his eyes it wouldn't be long till she would hear about it.

"Alicia, have you ever wondered what Jesus really meant when He said we should love our enemies? He admits that under the Old Law it was different, and there were times when God commanded Israel to annihilate their enemies. But He seems to be saying that things are different now. Listen to this:

> You have heard that it was said, 'You shall love your neighbor and hate your enemy.' But I say to you, love your enemies, bless those who curse you, do good to those who hate you, and pray for those who spitefully use you and persecute you, that you may be sons of your Father in heaven; for He makes His sun rise on the evil and on the good, and sends rain on the just and on the unjust. For if you love those who love you, what reward have you? Do not even the tax collectors do the same? And if you greet your brethren only, what

do you do more than others? Do not even the tax collectors do so?"[1]

They sat for a moment trying to let the impact of these words sink in. On the one hand they were very simple words, easy to understand. Just love others and do good to everyone who does evil to you. Jeremy could remember Mrs. Mulligan, his Sunday school teacher, using this passage and reminding the class that Jesus wanted them to be kind to each other.

But Jesus had not been teaching a Sunday school class. He had addressed fathers, mothers, shopkeepers, and . . . wait a minute. Could Roman soldiers have been listening in as well? How might they have received this message? Jeremy scratched his head as he pondered that. He knew from history that the Roman army was a powerful military machine. How could they function while living out this teaching? He remembered the words of John the Baptist when the soldiers had asked him what they should do. "Do violence to no man,"[2] John had told them.

Jeremy had already learned that Jesus' teachings were not easy, that many followers had walked away,

[1] Matthew 5:43–47
[2] Luke 3:14 (KJV)

and that following Jesus would cost a man every-thing. Jesus had been very clear on this. That pas-sage was a shocker, and Jeremy went back to look at it again.

> If anyone comes to Me and does not hate his father and mother, wife and children, brothers and sisters, yes, and his own life also, he cannot be My disciple. And who-ever does not bear his cross and come after Me cannot be My disciple.[3]

And then a few verses later;

> So likewise, whoever of you does not for-sake all that he has cannot be My disciple.[4]

Obviously Jesus would accept only total surren-der and loyalty. Jeremy's interest in history sparked his next questions. *So, what did the early Christians do with these teachings? How did they actually live them out?*

Jeremy stopped in that day at the university's li-brary. He wanted to know what those early believ-ers did with these radical teachings, and he found a tremendous amount of material. Every day after

---

[3] Luke 14:26–27
[4] Luke 14:33

classes were finished, he stopped in and explored the writings of the earliest believers, some of whom had been taught by the Apostles themselves. He found that not only were Christians during the first two hundred years opposed to fighting, they were famous for their stand. It was one of their trademarks!

Justin Martyr, in a letter written to the Roman emperor around A.D. 165, said, "We who formerly used to murder one another now refrain from making war, even on our enemies."[i] And Justin Martyr was not alone. Jeremy discovered that all the early Christians, including the Apostles, were unanimous—followers of Jesus do not fight!

Jeremy paced the room as he tried to sort through this concept. All his life he had assumed that Christianity and military service were compatible. In fact, some of the most aggressive and militaristic politicians also claimed to be Christians! He needed time to think about this.

Jeremy turned back to the Gospel of John and reread some words that had previously perplexed him. "My kingdom is not of this world," Jesus had said. "If My kingdom were of this world, My servants would fight."[5] Jesus was admitting that there

---

5 John 18:36

is more than one kingdom, and saying that His doesn't fight.

A kingdom that doesn't fight? That would be a different kingdom! Jeremy's mind flashed back over

scenes of fighting in the Middle East. He pictured the bloodshed, children left parentless, and devastated villages left behind. He was well aware of the impact a kingdom that used guns and bombs had in the world, and it certainly wasn't peaceful! But what if a kingdom's primary weapon was love? How would this work, and what kind of impact would this kind of kingdom have on the world?

Jesus talked a lot about this kingdom of God. What did He mean? Whatever it was, this kingdom was close to His heart. Doing a quick word search, Jeremy found that Jesus referred to it almost one hundred times. Amazing! Jesus said much more about the kingdom than other important topics like salvation, prayer, or the new birth.

Jeremy had never realized Jesus spoke so much about His kingdom! What might the world look like today if the church had retained its original stance of loving its enemies?

Jeremy thought back to his oath of enlistment when he joined the army. He was asked to pledge his total allegiance to the United States of America. As Jeremy read the history of the early church, he realized this was exactly how they viewed becoming a part of Jesus' kingdom. When they stated their faith in Jesus, repented of their sins, and asked for water baptism, they were pledging their allegiance to the kingdom of God. Unconditional allegiance! Many of them lost their lives simply because they chose to join this kingdom that wouldn't fight.

Reaching over to his page titled "Questions for Pastor Mike," Jeremy added the third item to his list.

1. If a man's works do not matter, then why does the Bible say we will be judged by them?

2. Why do we teach and focus so much on personal happiness and so little on personal holiness?

3. Why does the church no longer teach that followers of Jesus should love their enemies, live defenseless lives, and not participate in war?

CHAPTER SIX

MARRIAGE FOR LIFE?

Returning home from Bible study one Wednesday evening, Alicia seemed quiet. It was obvious she was preoccupied, so Jeremy finally inquired what was bothering her.

"After the meeting a few of us ladies were talking, and one of them mentioned that Pastor Mike has been dating Megan Johnson."

"Why would that bother you? He has been an eligible bachelor for a long time. What is wrong with him finally starting to look around?"

"But Megan has just recently divorced. Jesus didn't have much good to say about divorce."

"What did the other ladies say?" asked Jeremy, heading for the refrigerator for a drink of lemonade.

"Oh, there were differences of opinion. Some thought that since they were both good Christians there was nothing wrong with it. Others said he should at least wait until the papers were filed. One said it isn't right for any couples to divorce and remarry unless they were unbelievers when they divorced."

Alicia walked into the living room and dropped into a chair before continuing. "It's just confusing to me. Nobody seemed to have any Scripture verses to back what she was saying, and yet each was sure she was right."

Jeremy took a long drink and thought for a bit. "Jesus did talk about it, but I am not sure what all He said. How about studying the topic with me over the next few days? Let's just start looking for all the verses dealing with divorce and marriage and try to discern God's heart on this issue."

The next several days found Jeremy and Alicia reading, discussing, and writing down their findings. They started back in the Old Testament, noting the places where the Mosaic Law dealt with the topic. Then they dug into the gospels where Jesus clearly addressed marriage, divorce, and remarriage.

"This reminds me of my study about how to regard my enemies," remarked Jeremy one evening toward the end of their search. "It seems there was some allowance for divorce under the Old Law. But then Jesus comes along and says it's going to be different from now on. Listen to this:

> It has been said, Whosoever shall put away his wife, let him give her a writing of divorcement: but I say unto you, That whosoever shall put away his wife, except for the cause of fornication, causes her to commit adultery: and whosoever shall marry her that is divorced commits adultery."[1]

"That doesn't give much room for divorce," said Alicia as she flipped pages in search of a verse she had seen earlier. "That sounds like a man can divorce his wife only if she has been involved in immorality, but the woman can't ever remarry. That one seems to leave one small loophole for the man, but listen to what Jesus says here:

> Whoever divorces his wife and marries another commits adultery against her. And if a woman divorces her husband and marries another, she commits adultery."[2]

"Wow, God is pretty serious about marriage!

---

[1] Matthew 5:31–32 (KJV 2000)

[2] Mark 10:11–12

There's no loophole in that statement! But, Alicia, why don't we hear anything about this at church? We have many members who have been remarried. Why is this topic avoided?"

"I don't know. We hear a lot about homosexuality, but nothing regarding divorce. But it seems the Bible has more verses regarding divorce than about same-sex relationships." They sat in silence for a few minutes. What were they to do with all this information? They had agreed to continue being an encouragement at Lakeside, but what if they started sharing their findings? How would their friends react if they verbalized what Jesus said regarding a divorced individual remarrying while his or her spouse was still living?

During the next few days Jeremy used his study time in the university library to read up on how the early church dealt with divorce. He searched for articles written immediately after the New Testament writings and once again found those early believers very consistent. Justin Martyr stated the church's position simply: "All who by human law are twice married are in the eye of our Master sinners."[i]

Tertullian later wrote of Jesus' commands on this topic and explained it this way: "In order to forbid divorce, He makes it unlawful to marry a woman that has been put away."[ii]

Jeremy did an exhaustive search, and at the conclusion there was no doubt. The message of Jesus, the New Testament epistles, and the historic writings of the early church were consistent and clear. God intends that marriage be between one man and one woman, and this commitment is to be until death. Jeremy could find no exceptions. When divorce did occur, the believer was expected to live single.

As he reviewed his findings, he soberly realized that the current confusion in the American church regarding this issue was not due to a lack of information. God's position regarding marriage, divorce, and remarriage was clear. Once again Jeremy opened his tablet to the page titled "Questions for Pastor Mike" and added his fourth question to the list.

1. If a man's works do not matter, then why does the Bible say we will be judged by them?

2. Why do we teach and focus so much on personal happiness and so little on personal holiness?

3. Why does the church no longer teach that followers of Jesus should love their enemies, live defenseless lives, and not participate in war?

4. What happened to Jesus' teaching and the church's historic position regarding divorce and remarriage?

CHAPTER SEVEN

MONEY, POSSESSIONS, AND JESUS

Coming into Lakeside's main entrance one Sunday morning, Jeremy noticed a small display of brochures he hadn't seen before. Curious, he picked one up, stuck it in his Bible, and promptly forgot about it. That evening while thinking about the morning message, he opened his Bible and the brochure fell out. Jeremy quickly skimmed the material.

"Alicia, maybe this is what we need. There is a seminar coming up called 'Building Wealth God's Way.' I have been wondering if we could use a little help with our finances. They are planning to have sessions on getting ahead financially and planning now for the retirement of your dreams. Should we sign up?"

Leaving the snack she had been preparing in the kitchen, Alicia came into the living room and sat down. She didn't respond immediately, and something was obviously on her mind. "I didn't say anything the other night when you were reading aloud from one of the gospels, but I noticed something I have been thinking about ever since. Have you noticed how much Jesus talked about money and wealth?"

"Well," replied Jeremy, looking again at the brochure, "do you think that is what they will address at this seminar? I've noticed various places where Jesus talked about money and wealth, but I just glossed over those verses because I didn't know what to do with them."

"But, Jeremy, isn't that what most of us have been doing? When we find something Jesus said that doesn't agree with our lifestyle, we either go around it or find an explanation that allows us to feel good without changing. But Jesus said some things in the Sermon on the Mount that are very different from how I normally think of money. And what about Jesus telling that rich young ruler to give up everything to follow Him? Why would He say that?"

"I don't know, Alicia, but let's not get too carried away. I've heard Pastor Mike say that this rich man was just too attached to his money. Maybe he was a special case."

While eating their snack, Jeremy and Alicia continued discussing and trying to wrap their minds around Jesus' message regarding money and wealth. As they searched, Jeremy suddenly gave a low whistle.

"Wow! I know we read this before, but listen:

> Do not lay up for yourselves treasures on earth, where moth and rust destroy and where thieves break in and steal; but lay up for yourselves treasures in heaven, where neither moth nor rust destroys and where thieves do not break in and steal. For where your treasure is, there your heart will be also."[1]

Both sat for a moment pondering the words before Alicia broke the silence. "Obviously Jesus wasn't too excited about people trying to amass wealth. We commonly hear it is okay to have wealth as long as your heart isn't affected. But Jesus said that your treasure and your heart will be in the same place, and you can't have wealth without it affecting your heart. How does all this

---

[1] Matthew 6:19–21

apply to our lives? What did the first believers do with these radical teachings?"

Alicia chuckled as she headed back to the kitchen. "It looks like we have more to research this coming week!"

It didn't take Jeremy and Alicia long to discover that those early Christians were serious about applying Jesus' teachings to their money and possessions. Just as Jesus didn't shy away from the topic, they didn't either. In fact, judging from the book of Acts, possessions seemed to be one of the first things affected by a person's decision to follow Jesus.

"Think about what this is saying, Alicia!

> Now all who believed were together, and had all things in common, and sold their possessions and goods, and divided them among all, as anyone had need."[2]

Jeremy turned a couple of pages and continued. "And just after they got in trouble for preaching about Jesus, it says:

> And with great power the apostles gave witness to the resurrection of the Lord Jesus. And great grace was upon them all.

[2] Acts 2:44–45

Nor was there anyone among them who lacked; for all who were possessors of lands or houses sold them, and brought the proceeds of the things that were sold, and laid them at the apostles' feet; and they distributed to each as anyone had need."[3]

Alicia glanced back over at the "Building Wealth God's Way" brochure. "I can't see the Apostles giving seminars with those titles! Those first believers didn't just talk about Jesus' warnings regarding wealth, they actually did something about it!"

Jeremy put down his pen and looked over at Alicia. "They took the basic teachings of Jesus and put them into action. They didn't sit around and figure out some theological way to keep living as they had been and still feel good about it. Maybe that is why it's called the book of Acts! But I wonder how long the church kept this view of wealth and possessions?"

---

[3] Acts 4:33–35

Jeremy went back to the historical writings written by believers just after the New Testament was written. He discovered men like Clement of Alexandria. Clement was a powerful and prolific writer who addressed issues facing new believers coming from pagan backgrounds. One of his writings, written around 200 A.D., was titled *Who Is the Rich Man That Shall Be Saved?* Jeremy found this work to be practical and loyal to Jesus' teachings.

All of the early writers were consistent. They believed there was great danger in wealth, that money and possessions have been given by God for us to share, and that a follower of Jesus will not desire to accumulate riches. And again, they weren't content just talking about what Jesus said.

"Alicia, listen to this. Cyprian was a wealthy Roman, and when he became a believer, he took the teachings of Jesus seriously. He saw wealth, like Jesus had said, as a hindrance to a man's spiritual life. Consequently, Cyprian liquidated his estate and gave the money to the poor. As a pastor he then devoted his life to the church. He was finally beheaded for his faith in A.D. 258. These early believers were serious! They were so excited about Jesus and so focused on His kingdom that they had no time for or interest in accumulating earthly wealth!"

Jeremy picked up the brochure again. He tried to picture Cyprian getting excited about attending sessions with titles like "Getting Ahead Financially," "How to Accumulate Wealth," or "Planning Now for the Retirement of Your Dreams." The thought was preposterous! These men had turned their backs on wealth, materialism, and the kingdom of this world.

Picking up his tablet, Jeremy once again turned to the page titled "Questions for Pastor Mike" and added a fifth question to the list.

1. If a man's works do not matter, then why does the Bible say we will be judged by them?

2. Why do we teach and focus so much on personal happiness and so little on personal holiness?

3. Why does the church no longer teach that followers of Jesus should love their enemies, live defenseless lives, and not participate in war?

4. What happened to Jesus' teaching and the church's historic position regarding divorce and remarriage?

5. Why don't we view wealth and possessions the same way Jesus and the early church did?

CHAPTER EIGHT

HAVE WE BEEN IMMUNIZED?

As Jeremy and Alicia compared the early church to Lakeside Believers Fellowship, they were sobered and alarmed. Both groups claimed Jesus Christ as their Savior, but there was little resemblance after that. And as Jeremy and Alicia reviewed and discussed the questions they had written down for Pastor Mike, they realized that these five questions only scraped the surface. When a man became a believer in the first couple of centuries after Christ, everything about his life needed to change.

In contrast, when a man decided to accept Jesus at Lakeside, little actual change was expected. After standing up some Sunday morning and sharing that he had accepted Jesus as his personal Savior, a man would continue living much as he had before except that he came to worship services and maybe joined a Bible study. In fact, if he, like Cyprian in the third century, suddenly sold all his unneeded assets and distributed them to the poor, people would become concerned about his sanity!

"The bottom line, Alicia, is this. When a man in the early church chose to follow Jesus, everything about that man was transformed. Today when a man accepts the Lord, very little changes."

Setting her coffee down, Alicia looked at Jeremy. "Did you notice what you just said? They chose to follow, and we just accept. Those early believers made a conscious and deliberate decision to obey Jesus regardless of the cost. In contrast, we talk of deciding to accept Him into our lives. How did we get from following Jesus to just accepting Him?"

"I think you're right. What we are saying, without necessarily realizing it, is that Jesus is strong enough to forgive our sins, but He doesn't give us enough power to actually live a daily counter-culture lifestyle of obedience to His teachings. Those first Christians believed Jesus was powerful enough to do both!"

Alicia considered Jeremy's statement and then took a sip of coffee before responding. "So what do we do now?"

"I'm not sure. I have a feeling that a good portion of our congregation wouldn't be interested in what we're discovering."

Jeremy set his Bible on the coffee table and lay back in his recliner. "Alicia, do you remember learning in school how vaccines work? Smallpox was defeated because Edward Jenner made a brilliant discovery. He found that if someone could overcome a tiny dose of cowpox, that person became immune to a larger infection of smallpox. So he began injecting people with a small dose, and from then on they were immune. It almost seems the same principle applies to Christianity in America."

"I'm not following you. Explain what you mean."

"The church in America is familiar with Jesus' death on the cross, His resurrection, and the fact that His blood cleanses us from sin. But that's just part of the story. The Christianity of the Bible was so much greater! They taught that Jesus not only forgives our sins, but also grants us power to overcome sin and obey Him in our daily lives. Their Gospel was powerful enough to transform men!"

Jeremy got out of his chair and began pacing as he continued, excited with this new thought. "But

we seem to be inoculated. It's as though we have received a small dose of Christianity, and the little we
have received has inoculated us against the com-
plete Gospel that Jesus died to give us. We have
been vaccinated, and now the power of the Gospel
that Jesus intended would change our lives has little
impact. Maybe
that's why we
struggle.

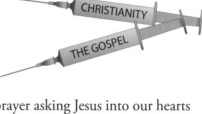

"We have
been taught
that offering a prayer asking Jesus into our hearts
makes us Christians. We can continue to live a
comfortable American lifestyle and enjoy all the
entertainment the world has to offer, yet be confident that we will go to heaven when we die. And
we like that arrangement! But if Jesus meant what
He said, what we have been told isn't true!"

"I agree that there is a tremendous difference
between the two messages," Alicia said. "Jesus repeatedly warned that following Him would be difficult and affect every part of our lives, and that if
we weren't willing to take up our cross and follow
Him, we couldn't be His disciples.[1] So how did

---

[1] Matthew 10:34–39; Matthew 16:24–25; Mark 8:34–35; Luke 9:23–24;
Luke 14:25–33

the church get from where it was in the first few centuries to where it is today?"

"I don't know, Alicia. But I am convinced of one thing. What we have today is not what Jesus originally intended. And in light of Jesus' teachings and strong warnings, we cannot afford to stop searching. If I'm wrong, I want to find out now, not after I die. Jesus promised that those who seek will find.[2] Let's continue seeking, fasting, and praying for spiritual discernment."

[2] Luke 11:9–10

CHAPTER NINE

WHAT HAPPENED TO THE POWER?

Jeremy and Alicia are fictional characters in an imaginary church, but they represent many sincere seekers in America today. As the author, I don't know what your experience with Christianity has been, what you have been taught, or whether you can relate to Jeremy and Alicia's situation. But before moving on, I want to ask you a question: "Is it possible that you have received a small dose and have been inoculated against true Christianity?"

Maybe you have found Jesus and have indisputable evidence that He has worked in your life. You know you were lost, were on a downward path, and through the redeeming power of Jesus have found peace and joy. But have you considered the possibility that God may have more in store for you? It may be that the little taste you have had is inoculating you from further blessing.

These questions are not designed to create unnecessary doubt. Rather, they are intended to help you examine your faith. And the reason all professing Christians need to examine their faith is simple. Jesus said that many people who sincerely believe they are saved will end up in hell. Notice this profound yet largely overlooked warning:

> Not everyone who says to Me, "Lord, Lord," shall enter the kingdom of heaven, but he who does the will of My Father in heaven. Many will say to Me in that day, "Lord, Lord, have we not prophesied in Your name, cast out demons in Your name, and done many wonders in Your name?" And then I will declare to them, "I never knew you; depart from Me, you who practice lawlessness!"[1]

Can you grasp the weight of those words? Picture the scene for a moment. The Bible says the Day of Judgment will come, and at this great event every person's life will be examined.[2] Each of us will stand before God. But the sobering fact is that many will come assuming they had been saved,

---

[1] Matthew 7:21–23

[2] Matthew 25:32; 2 Corinthians 5:10

even though they hadn't been following Jesus at all. They died, confident that they were redeemed by the blood of Jesus and were saved, when in fact they weren't. They may have attended church, led a Bible study, or even pastored a church. But when they came before God, they were not prepared.

I don't believe Jesus gave this sobering glimpse into the end of time to cause mental turmoil, uncertainty, or a lack of assurance in our relationship with Him. He wants us to be prepared! And He gave concise instructions on how to do that. He said that a wise man will prepare for that day by hearing His teachings and doing them.[3]

This truth is rarely heard, let alone emphasized, in most churches today. In fact, just suggesting that Jesus intended for us to live out His teachings will probably label you as a legalist—someone trying to be saved by good works. So what did those first Christians actually believe about obedience?

The early church fully understood that their own works were insufficient for salvation. This is clear from the epistles and the writings we have access to from the next two hundred years. The Apostle Paul numerous times established the fact that no

---

[3] Matthew 7:24

one would be saved by doing enough good apart from Christ.[4] Cyprian, that early believer who gave his wealth to the poor, did not believe that good works apart from Jesus would merit salvation. In explaining the centrality of Jesus in salvation, he wrote, "It is impossible to reach the Father except by His Son Jesus Christ."[i] Men like Cyprian understood the importance of the blood of Jesus and the hopelessness of trying to earn merit with God without His grace. But they also knew that God is more interested in how we live than in what we say.

God has always desired a loving relationship with His people. Was God's ultimate goal under the Old Law to have a people who killed animals correctly and at the proper time? Did He really take pleasure in lots of dead livestock and blood all over the altar? Of course not. He wanted a people who loved Him and wanted a relationship with Him. Those early Christians understood that God wants a relationship with His creation. And they understood they couldn't have that relationship without obeying what He said.

Our religious culture has provided us with a false dilemma. We are taught that a man must choose

---

[4] Romans 3:20; Ephesians 2:8–9; 2 Timothy 1:9

between salvation by faith and trying to be saved by our works. A man who attempts to obey Jesus is accused of trying to merit salvation. But those first believers in Jerusalem wouldn't have understood this theological dichotomy. They believed that salvation was a gift purchased by Jesus Christ on the cross when He paid the ransom for our sins. But they also believed this gift was conditional.

In other words, God can give this gift to anyone He chooses. And He chooses to bestow this gift on anyone who has faith in Him, repents of past sins, is baptized with water, and chooses to follow Jesus in daily life through the power of the Holy Spirit. It isn't a complicated process or a complex theology. But it does require the surrender of one's will and a commitment to follow Jesus in daily life.

Those first Christians believed in a powerful Gospel. Lives were transformed, and the Roman world was turned upside down. The Roman army cowered before this kingdom that didn't fight. After all, how could they threaten men who didn't fear death?

So what has happened to the Christianity that was powerful enough to cause men to give away their fortunes, face lions in the stadiums, and sing while being burned at the stake? Why did we ever exchange a Gospel powerful enough to change men's lives for one that simply makes them comfortable with who they are? These are good questions, and there are answers in history. But we must understand that the popular, feel-good Christianity promoted today would have been foreign to those early believers.

CHAPTER TEN

DID JESUS REALLY SAY THAT?

Thankfully there are a growing number of "Jeremy and Alicias" in our day who are waking up and starting to take the words of Jesus seriously. They are seeking the Lord and committing themselves to follow Jesus' teachings. But what about you? Analyze your own walk with God. Do you really believe Jesus meant what He said? Let's look at some truths that Jesus was clear about. There are more, but here are a few statements that anyone who is serious about following Jesus should be able to say:

1. Obedience to the commands of Jesus is not optional.

This truth is all through the New Testament. We are saved by grace through faith. But God has promised this grace to those who choose to obey Him.[1] Repeatedly the Bible reminds us how important it is to obey God. We are told that only those who are obedient will be in heaven,[2] that those who continue in sin will be condemned to hell,[3] and that ultimately we will be judged by our works.[4] There is a staggering amount of teaching telling us that how we live our daily lives is extremely important, yet in spite of this evidence many are teaching the exact opposite.

2. God is much more concerned about personal holiness than personal happiness.

God not only commands us to be holy,[5] but He also promises us the power to do what He asks.[6] God knows our weakness and is willing to forgive when we fail,[7] but His ultimate goal is that we do not sin.[8] In our day, grace has been distorted. Grace was not intended to eliminate

---

[1] Hebrews 5:9
[2] Matthew 7:21
[3] John 5:29
[4] Matthew 16:27
[5] 1 Peter 1:15–17
[6] Acts 1:8; John 15:5; 1 John 3:9
[7] 1 John 1:9
[8] 1 John 2:1

the need for good works.[9] Rather, it abolishes the need for sin. No longer do we need to be held in bondage by Satan to the power of sin. Through the power of the resurrected Jesus, we not only have forgiveness of sin, but we also have the power to live holy, victorious lives of good works!

3. Jesus' primary focus was the kingdom of God, and its citizens do not fight.

If you ask most Christians what the primary theme of Jesus' teaching was, you will most likely hear about man's need for salvation or the importance of the new birth. These are important topics, but Jesus spent far more time teaching about the kingdom of God than any other topic. This primary focus of Jesus' teaching is rarely referred to in modern preaching. Jesus taught that His kingdom is a present reality on earth, and that His servants do not fight.[10] Many followers of Jesus have lived defenseless lives throughout history, and many have chosen to die rather than take up arms.

---

[9] Titus 2:11–14
[10] John 18:36; Matthew 5:44

4. Divorce and remarriage, regardless of what culture teaches, is still wrong.

Jesus' words are clear. "Whoever divorces his wife and marries another commits adultery against her. And if a woman divorces her husband and marries another, she commits adultery."[11] Yet amazingly, it is difficult to find a pastor today who will not compromise on this basic teaching when pressed. All kinds of excuses are made. "He wasn't a believer when he was first married" or, "Asking them to live separately would be too difficult."

These are difficult issues, and sometimes the solutions are painful. But Jesus never promised that following Him would be easy, and many men and women have chosen to live single because of their circumstances. They found consolation in the promise that Jesus would be with them to the end.[12] And imagine how much more credibility the church would have today when confronting issues like homosexuality if it had been faithful to Jesus' teachings regarding divorce and remarriage!

---

[11] Mark 10:11–12

[12] Matthew 28:20

5. Wealth makes following Jesus extremely difficult.

Jesus said, "It is easier for a camel to go through the eye of a needle than for a rich man to enter the kingdom of God."[13] This is a powerful statement, but looking around at American Christianity, you would think Jesus had never opened His mouth on this topic. Far from being discouraged, the pursuit of wealth is lauded and encouraged. Wealthy businessmen are admired and find a place of prominence in the church today. Telling them what Jesus actually taught about wealth could be costly. True followers of Jesus will work diligently, not to accumulate wealth, but to help those in need.[14]

Where Do I Go from Here?

Maybe some of the thoughts in this book have frustrated you. Perhaps you are ready to toss this little book aside and forget it. But before you do, I challenge you to take another look at the teachings of the Man we claim to follow.

Since the time Jesus lived here, men have wrestled with His teachings. Some have chosen to

---

[13] Matthew 19:24
[14] Ephesians 4:28

examine them from an academic, theological position. They debate His words, wonder if He intended them to be taken literally, and sometimes create theological arguments that actually negate His teachings.

Others just assume they are following Jesus while giving little thought to what He actually said. Like those at 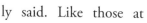 Lakeside Believers Fellowship, they attend church and use the lifestyles and teachings of their pastors to determine the criteria for being a Christian. Instead of following Jesus, they follow those who claim to follow Him.

But throughout church history there have always been groups of people who have taken Jesus' words seriously and tried to follow them. While acknowledging their dependence on God's grace and their need of cleansing through Jesus' blood, they believe that God imparts this grace and forgiveness alone to those who choose to love and obey Him.

I challenge you to take a closer look at the words of Jesus. Like Jeremy and Alicia, take the time to pray, fast, and seriously consider what Jesus taught. Read what He said with a desire to apply His teachings, regardless of the cost. And remember, only those who seek and follow Jesus wholeheartedly will find the true joy that comes from obedience.

If you have questions or would like to locate other followers of Jesus who are serious about doing what He says, please contact kingdomquestions@gmail.com.

ENDNOTES

Chapter Five

i *The First Apology of Justin,* Justin Martyr, The Ante-Nicene Fathers, Eerdmans Publishing Company, Grand Rapids, Michigan, reprint 1989, Vol. I, p. 176.

Chapter Six

i Ibid., p. 167.
ii Ibid., Vol. III, p. 404.

Chapter Nine

i *The Treatises of Cyprian*, The Ante-Nicene Fathers, Eerdmans Publishing Company, Grand Rapids, Michigan, reprint 1989, Vol. V, p. 542.

RESOURCES FOR FURTHER STUDY

If you would like to learn more about these topics or more regarding the early Christians, here are some additional resources you may want to consider.

The Kingdom That Turned the World Upside Down, *David Bercot*

This is an excellent work on the early church, their love for the kingdom of God, and how their devotion to Jesus impacted the Roman world. If you are serious about seeking God and learning about the early church, this is an extremely good resource.

The Upside-Down Kingdom, *Donald B. Kraybill*

The author explores the Lordship of Jesus and how it should affect His people. It is a study of the kingdom of God through the synoptic gospels and contrasts the kingdom of this world with the kingdom of God.

What the Bible Says About Divorce and Remarriage, *John Coblentz*

This book takes a close look at Jesus' actual words regarding divorce. It is written with compassion for those who find themselves in difficult situations, and looks for solutions that agree with what Jesus said on this topic.

A Change of Allegiance, *Dean Taylor*

The author and his wife were both enlisted in the U.S. Army when they began to realize what Jesus said about loving their enemies. This is a good first-hand account of two people who seriously looked at applying the teachings of Jesus to their lives, knowing that choosing to follow would be costly. An excellent book to better understand the two kingdoms and defenseless living.

A Dictionary of Early Christian Beliefs, *David Bercot*

This dictionary can be helpful in learning what the early Christians believed regarding specific topics. Topics are in alphabetical order, and quotes are used so you can see what these early believers believed about each subject.

ABOUT THE AUTHOR

Gary Miller was raised in California and today lives with his wife Patty and family in the Pacific Northwest. Gary works with the poor in developing countries and directs the SALT Microfinance Solutions program for Christian Aid Ministries. This program offers business and spiritual teaching to those living in chronic poverty, provides small loans, sets up local village savings groups, and assists them in learning how to use their God-given resources to become sustainable.

ADDITIONAL RESOURCES

BY GARY MILLER

BOOKS

Kingdom-Focused Finances for the Family

This first book in the Kingdom-Focused Living series is realistic, humorous, and serious about getting us to become stewards instead of owners.

Charting a Course in Your Youth

A serious call to youth to examine their faith, focus, and finances. Second book in Kingdom-Focused Living series.

Going Till You're Gone

A plea for godly examples—for older men and women who will demonstrate a kingdom-focused vision all the way to the finish line. Third book in Kingdom-Focused Living series.

The Other Side of the Wall

Stresses Biblical principles that apply to all Christians who want to reflect God's heart in giving. Applying these principles has the potential to change lives— first our own, and then the people God calls us to share with. Fourth book in Kingdom-Focused Living series.

It's Not Your Business

How involved in business should followers of Jesus be? Did God intend the workplace to play a prominent role in building His kingdom? Explore the benefits and dangers in business. Fifth and final book in the Kingdom-Focused Living series.

Budgeting Made Simple

A budgeting workbook in a ring binder; complements *Kingdom-Focused Finances for the Family*.

What Happened to Our Money?

Ignorance of Biblical money management can set young people on a path of financial hardship that results in anxiety, marital discord, depression, and envy. This short book presents young couples with foundational truths on which to build their financial lives.

Life in a Global Village

Would your worldview change if the world population were shrunk to a village of one hundred people and you lived in that village? Full-color book.

This Side of the Global Wall

Pictures and graphs in this full-color book portray the unprecedented opportunities Americans have today. What are we doing with the resources God has given us?